Living the Prudent Life

Baltazar Gracian Morales

Living
the
Prudent Life

The Timeless Wisdom
of Baltazar Gracian

ASTROLOG PUBLISHING HOUSE LTD

Baltazar Gracian Morales

Living the Prudent Life
The Timeless Wisdom of Baltazar Gracian

Translated by Juan de-Aragon
Language Consultant: Carole de-Paz
Editor: Elisha Ben Mordechai

© Astrolog Publishing House 2012

P. O. Box 1123, Hod Hasharon 45111, Israel
TEL. 972-9-7412044
FAX. 972-9-7442714
E-Mail: sarabm@netvision.net.il
Astrolog Web Site: www.astrolog.co.il

ISBN 978-965-494-350-5

All rights reserved. No part of this publication may be reproduced, stored in a retrieval system, or transmitted, in any form or by any means, electronic, mechanical, photocopying, recording or otherwise, without the prior permission of the publisher.

Published by Astrolog Publishing House 2012

APHORISMS OF WORDLY WISDOM

Baltazar Gracian Morales [portrait 1640]

INTRODUCTION

Baltazar Gracian Morales was born on the 8th day of January 1601 in a village in Lamontana in the County of Aragon in Spain — the son of a physician who was raised and educated in his uncle's — the pastor — house.

He studied at a Jesuit school for three years (from 1616 to 1619) and then went to Saragossa for religious studies. In 1627 he joined the Jesuit Order and in 1635 took his vows and began teaching at various Jesuit schools.

A short time later, Gracian was published as a preacher, and a number of his sermons were printed through funding of a wealthy patron, and were widely distributed. These sermons, dealing mainly with moral behavior, were selected and edited for this book *Living the Prudent Life*. In 1640, Gracian became renowned as a preacher in Madrid and in 1646 he serves as an army chaplain in the Spanish army that fought against the French.

In 1651, Gracian printed the first volume of a book called *Things That Need to Be Corrected* without the sanction of his superiors, and six years later published — despite opposition — the third

volume. As a result, he was punished and banished to Graus. He tried, without success, to leave the Jesuit Order. He died in 1658 and was buried in Tarragona which is near Saragossa in Aragon County.

Baltazar Gracian is the most typical representative of the style of the "Conceptors" in the period known as the Spanish Baroque literature, and his books are the most well-known literary heritage of the Baroque period in Spain. His writings influenced a long line of philosophers and meditative thinkers — among whom are Le Roschpechot, Voltaire, Nietzsche and Schopenhauer.

Gracian was, in his lifetime, so famous that the village where he was born changed its name to Belmonte De Gracian in his honor.

With the help of Juan de Aragon 800 meditations relating to young people, either directly or indirectly — the audience that Gracian would most often address — were collected. Elisha Ben Mordechai, an author and editor in a publishing house, selected around 207 meditations that appeal to the young hearts of today and presents them in appropriate language.

Living the Prudent Life

1

Being like others is the way of the world.

Being like others is the way of the world —
a paved way with no ups or downs.
Being an individual is the path of the
unique man — a narrow path that twists
through mountains and valleys and holds
many obstacles that trip him up.
The crossroads — between the paved way and
the winding path is before you — and it is the
right and duty of each individual (including the
younger person) to choose between the two.

2

A young man fills his cup to overflowing.

A young man fills his cup to overflowing, his plate till it's heaped, his stomach to bursting and drinks to oblivion. And the way he behaves to his body is the way he behaves with his beliefs, in his life and his emotions — filling each vessel to overflowing.
The older man has learned the importance of emptiness — he'll always leave room in his glass, on his plate and in his body so that he can fully embrace the unexpected. Most importantly, he leaves space in his beliefs.
And so, if the young man were to hear messages of God, they would not get through to his heart, whereas the old man's heart will always have room to receive them.

3

The most beautiful flower.

The most beautiful flower, the most breathtaking view, the beauty in the perfect work of art — all these are only shadows of the Divine source from which everything comes!

4

On one bitter winter's day.

On one bitter winter's day, the community found the body of a beggar woman who had died from the cold and damp in her shack. While bearing her body to burial, people murmured, "Woe, how bitter is the fate of a person who doesn't have God's light."
Only an old man lagging behind the coffin mumbled, "How bitter is the fate of a person whose neighbors didn't see his plight because they were blinded by God's glory."

5

One of the ancient kings.

One of the ancient kings, Labarnache the First who ruled the Hittite Kingdom, was looking for a commander-in-chief for his army.
He placed a beggar in tattered clothes at the entrance to his castle and invited the soldiers of his army to apply for the post (this was the way it was done by the Hittites). And so it was, every day the King would sit on the castle porch and watch all the candidates coming — and would send them away immediately.
Until, finally, an unknown unranked soldier arrived carrying a spear and entered the gates. The King immediately went down to greet him and hugged him, declaring him his commander-in-chief.
The embarrassed soldier mumbled that he was there only for his shift and that he wasn't deserving of the rank... but the King placed the commander-in-chief scepter in his hands — and a King's order, in the Hittite Kingdom, was like an order of god.

With the passing of the days the simple soldier became the highest commander of the kingdom, the one who widened the borders of the kingdom from the Black Sea to the River Nile. The King, who was already old, lay on his deathbed.

His oldest son and heir to the throne then asked, "Father, there is one thing you didn't teach me — how did you choose a simple soldier to be the commander-in-chief of the greatest army in the world?"

His father replied, "Ahh, that is very simple. He was the only one that bowed his head in greeting to the beggar sitting at the entrance..."

Therefore, when you are looking for the strongest man in a very big crowd, look for the politest one in deed and manner.

6

The burning log.

The burning log that warms the house today,
is the ash that will fertilize the field tomorrow.

7

The young person believes.

The young person believes that he can pay his debts with sweet words.
But this is not so — even if he has honey under his tongue and a sack full of Thessalian magic (thought to be the source of all magic), he will still have to learn that he can only pay his debts with money or items worth money.
Learn this and be a man.

8

The son of a woodchopper.

The son of a woodchopper who lived on the edge of the Black Forest was a rebellious youth who caused his parents much sorrow. He would curse non-stop, offend people and quarrel with the entire community.
One day, his father handed him a bucket filled with nails and a hammer, and led him into the forest. There was, in the depth of the forest, an oak tree with a very thick trunk. The father instructed his son to hammer seven nails into the tree trunk every time he offended someone, by word or by deed, and to pull out one nail every time he did a good deed — even if it was just avoiding hurting someone.
For many days the youngster would go into the depths of the forest and hammer into the tree trunk nail after nail until his temper calmed down. He them started to return to the tree trunk and remove nail after nail.
Months and years passed before he removed the last nail from the tree trunk.

On that day, the son — who was already a young man — invited his elderly father to go into the forest with him. They slowly walked the path to their destination and when they reached the tree, the son smiled.
"See, father, there isn't one nail in the tree trunk," he said proudly because despite his difficult character as a youth, he respected his father. "I learned the lesson!"
The old man ran his fingers along the tree trunk and said quietly, "Look, son, at the scars the nails have left in the tree trunk. Teach your son that a nail, even when it has been removed, leaves a mark for eternity..."

9

The wise man.

The wise man cleans and fixes the well while
it is full.
The stupid man fixes the well only when its water
has dried up.

10

The leaf that is carried away.

The leaf that is carried away by the wind is a dead leaf.
The fish that gets carried away by the stream is a dead fish.

11

The true shepherd.

The true shepherd leads his herd at the pace of the slowest sheep.
The careless shepherd leads his herd at the pace of the fastest sheep.

12

In Ancient Sardis.

In Ancient Sardis they wanted to elect a commander-in-chief who would lead the State's army. The King ordered that any soldier who wanted to be commander-in-chief write his name on a pebble and throw it into a deep hole. As there was a great number of soldiers in Sardis, the hole filled up quickly.

The King then sent his three-year-old son to fetch one of the pebbles from the hole and ruled that the name of the soldier that his son would bring back, would be the army's commander.

The King's ministers saw this and were fearful. They came before the King and claimed that this was not the way to choose a commander-in-chief, and each one gave a suggestion as to how to do so. This one claimed that the tallest soldier should be selected, the other said the oldest one should be and the next one argued that the archer who shot his arrow the furthest deserves to be chosen.

But the King cut short their objections and said, "I want a commander-in-chief with luck — that's more important for Sardis than anything else!"

13

One day, a townsman convinced his wife.

One day, a townsman convinced his wife to join him on a hike to the top of the mountain.
For many hours, the two climbed the mountain in the heat of the burning sun. When they reached the top, the man said to his wife:
"See how beautiful the view down below is."
"If the view is so beautiful down there, why did we have to climb all the way up here and get away from it?" asked the wife.

Philosophers and men of religion should learn from this woman's words.

14

Avoid the faults of your nation.

Avoid the faults of your nation.
Like water that shares the good or bad qualities of the earth through which it flows, so a young man shares the good or bad qualities of the nation into which he is born.
One person alone could never improve the flow of water in his country.
How can a nation improve its youngsters to nourish its future?
Are we to bring the youngsters water from hidden springs in tall mountains which is pure and clear and have yet to absorb the elements of the earth? Or do we, man and nation together, cleanse the earth so the water that runs water the youngsters with the good qualities
that are found within them?

15

The cleverest youth in the crowd.

The cleverest youth in the crowd is the one whose voice rises above all the other voices. But the cleverest among the aged is the old man whose words leave his mouth in a whisper that dies out as soon as it passes his cracked lips.

So the iron coin thrown into a metal box clatters and clangs on its journey down, while the sound of gold coins held in a leather pouch
are not heard.

16

A man and a woman.

A man and a woman are
the foundations of a house.
If you do not understand that,
saw off one of four table legs
and sit at that table to eat your meal...

17

In Latin.

In Latin, there are countless words for
"stupid"
and only few words for
"clever".

18

Many years ago three of Ancient Rome's wise men.

Many years ago three of Ancient Rome's wise men were sitting on the bank of the river eating their breakfast and bending each other's ear with their troubles.
"I have an only son who is as evil as they come," said the first wise man, "Daily I am summoned to the judge to pay for his misdeeds. He is ruining my life and my family's life. After considering the matter, I put him up in a small house on the border of my property and I blocked off the way to my house with a wall. Since then, I have not been damaged by his evildoings."
"I have one wife," sighed the second wise man, "and she deserves to be called one of the black plagues. All day and all night she would be on me like a stone until my days turned to nights and my nights became my deathbed. Until, in the end, I had had enough of her and I closed her up in a big house in my yard, and around it I built a wall and my servants bring her what she needs. Thus I returned my life to me."

"My neighbor is wicked," added the third wise man, "he sets his dogs on me, and he empties his slosh bucket on my doorstep. So I built a high wall around my house and the light came back into my life."

"Blessed be the wicked," murmured a worker who was sitting near them and heard their conversation while eating his breakfast. "If there wasn't evil and wickedness in the world, there wouldn't be a demand for high walls — whose construction has fed me and my household for many years..."

19

A good friend.

A good friend is man's treasure.
A bad friend is man's disaster.

20

The exaltation of the Caesar.

The exaltation of the Caesar,
the splendor of the King,
the brightness of the commander of the army,
the honor of the mayor...
None of these can stand against the blade
of the drawn sword.
But the spirit of the simple man, his honesty, will
stand forever.

Like him is the field of reeds that stays his
ground, bows his head and who, after the terrible
storm has passed, lifts his head while a forest of
lofty cedars falls to the ground in a storm.

21

When you cannot reach the top of the mountain.

When you cannot reach the top of the mountain on the path that you chose, you change the path, not the mountaintop.
When you cannot reach your goal, it is a mistake to alter your goal — the right way is to alter your path to the goal.

22

Look for the good.

Look for the good qualities within yourself,
and not within others.

23

The sun rises every dawn.

The sun rises every dawn
even if you do not greet it from
the roof of your house.
Night falls,
even if you do not close your eyes.
The grass grows in season,
the birds migrate on schedule
and schools of fish come to shore at set times.
This all happens — even if you do nothing.

24

A great difficulty that stands before the youth.

A great difficulty that stands before the youth is to learn and adjust to the habit of asking.
When you need your neighbor's horse to plow your field, learn to ask the neighbor for his horse.
I know that the thing that prevents the young man from asking is the fear that the answer will be negative. Nobody likes to hear "no"!
And the younger you are, the no sounds more reproving and hurtful to your ears.
But you must remember this, when you ask for your neighbor's horse, there are only two possible answers — "yes" or "no". And because it is the neighbor's horse, the "no" is very possible and the horse will not plow your field.
Ask.
If you are answered in the positive, go and plow your field. If you remain without, find another neighbor to ask.
My father would have added, never ask from another what you aren't willing to be asked of by another.

25

He who stands on his friend's shoulders.

He who stands on his friend's shoulders can easily
reach the fruit at the top of the tree.
A generation that stands on the older generation's
shoulders will have better vision.
As a ladder is built rung after rung,
so is the world —
step by step,
generation after generation.

26

It's better for the farmer.

It's better for the farmer to struggle with a stubborn mule than to carry the heavy sack on his own back.

27

Only a very few.

Only a very few would prefer a flawless polished pebble over a rough, flawed gemstone.

28

A kept secret.

A kept secret is like a closely guarded treasure. A secret that has been let out is like prison bars.

29

On a hot summer's day.

On a hot summer's day in Ancient Athens, a farmer called Mithradas knocked on his neighbor's door. When the door opened, Mithradas asked for the neighbor's horse. "What do you need it for?" asked the neighbor. "Yesterday, at the tavern, you promised to give me your horse as a gift," Mithradas said. "Yesterday I was so drunk I was under the table," the neighbor said. "In my drunkenness I was willing to give you all my property. Now that I'm sober and have a clear head, I am keeping my property."
But Mithradas persevered and took it to the local justice. He, after consideration, instructed the neighbor to take his horse to Mithradas' stable.

The moral is simple: Stick to one thing —
when you drink, drink!
When you talk, talk!
But never do both at the same time.

30

A young man's life.

A young man's life is a perpetual conflict with himself, with his father, with his mother, and so on. A young man may use the strategems of intention for weapons — never do what he seems to have a mind to do. He takes aim, 'tis true, but that only to deceive the eyes of those that look upon him.

But most of the youth are not like this. The innocence of youth guides them to mark the target at the beginning of the journey and to work towards it, even if the target is misguided, unattainable or clouded by the future.

This is the strength of the youth — and this is the trap that waits for them further down the path.

If an older man looks at the youth, in our confused world, he sees that all is not as it seems, but to the youth, all is as it seems.

31

A young maiden.

A young maiden, upon witnessing the actions of the older women in her family, in her village and in her country, says to herself, "I will be different!" This is the way of young maidens, but not the way of the world.
A young girl blossoms only when her ambitions and expectations are realized. But after that, she must bear the fruit — and then, and this is the way of the world, she behaves like those same women she criticized in her youth.

32

One Sunday morning.

One Sunday morning, as a youngster was walking with his uncle on a road that passed through villages, he noticed something glinting on the side of the road. Upon reaching it, he saw that it was a gold coin lying in the dust.
With great pride, he picked up the coin and showed it to his uncle.
"Uncle, now I can buy the flute that I want so much. Will you come with me to the shops and help me pick out a flute?"
His uncle didn't answer, but when the two reached the village, the youngster led them to the market.
At the first stall, the uncle and the youngster stopped and stared at the fresh fish that were laid out. The youngster stood near and waited. Finally, the uncle turned away from there and stopped at another stall, where he feasted his eyes upon the display of vegetables there.
From there, he went to a shop which displayed leather shoes at its front... and the youngster

followed him from shop to shop, from stall to stall until they reached the little shop which sold musical instruments.
"Now go," the uncle said to the youngster, "and buy yourself a flute at the price of the needs of the unhappy soul who lost his money."

33

The young man believes.

The young man believes that a young woman's beauty is measured by the softness of her hair, the smoothness of her complexion, her makeup and the color of her clothes.
With the passing of the years, he will learn that the only thing he needs to measure her beauty is the measure of love!

34

The young man gets to the village.

The young man gets to the village by the shortest route — jumping over fences, scrambling over rocks and getting wet in the streams he needs to cross. There isn't a time when he doesn't come home to his parents' house with tears in his clothes or wounds on his body.
The older man walks from his parents' house to the village on the paved road, crosses little wooden bridges and returns home without a sign of the road on him or on his clothes.

35

A kick in the young man's backside.

A kick in the young man's backside
is the best way of pushing him forward.

36

In a little village in the south of Spain.

In a little village in the south of Spain, in the valley between mountains covered in olive trees, lives a mute, hunchbacked man with an injured soul. He has never been seen sitting on the church pews, even though children in the community are forced to attend
all prayers and ceremonies.
Once, upon seeing the miserable man sitting on a rock in the field, a child asked his father,
"Why doesn't he have to come to prayers?"
The father berated his son on the question, but also answered it:
"Every time he sees the sunrise or the moon's halo, he sees the creator in front of his eyes much better than we can see ever him under the dome of drawings in the church."

37

The young boy who acts like an idiot.

The young boy who acts like an idiot and behaves
foolishly, deserves his father's admonitions;
and if he doesn't mend his ways,
his punishment will not be long in coming.
However, the young boy who acts like an idiot
and behaves foolishly with his whole being, and
does this in front of everybody without pause...
will be brought to the King's court and will
become the court jester, thus bestowing
great honor upon his father.

38

Every time a father took his son.

Every time a father took his son to the cobbler to buy him a new pair of shoes, he would stop next to a beggar with no legs who sat in the church doorway, and put a coin in his hand. And to this day, even as a grown man who is a father himself, when he wears shoes that press his feet, he doesn't complain because he remembers the beggar without legs sitting in the church doorway.

39

In my youth, as a holy servant.

In my youth, as a holy servant, I had to learn to brandish the sword and get the arrow on the target*. My teachers would always point out, "Each arrow that hits its target, is a salute to a hundred arrows that missed their target..."

*at that time whoever was ordained as a priest was permitted to carry a sword or weapon — a right that wasn't given to other subjects.

40

Bigger is the greatness of he who has failed.

Bigger is the greatness of he who has failed and got back on his feet, failed and got back up, than the greatness of one who reached his goal without any obstacles.

41

The best point to start.

The best point to start your life's journey is the one that's under your feet — at this very moment.

42

The dream is the only track.

The dream is the only track where you can gallop your horse without a bit and reins...

43

When you're angry.

When you're angry with your enemies,
remember the past.
When you're angry with your loved ones,
forget the past.

44

Even if you chop off the head of the snake.

Even if you chop off the head of the snake
that bit you,
you still need to go to the physician
to heal your wounds.

45

You will never be scowled at.

You will never be scowled at
if you give charity generously.

46

I was a youngster who has grown old.

I was a youngster who has grown old and I haven't forgotten the lesson that my father taught me. Every time the village parade passed by* my father would send me to smell the clothes of the boy who walked at the front of the parade and who carried the incense stick**, and then he would tell me to smell my sweat-soaked clothes. When I asked him the meaning of this, he answered, "See how pleasant the smell of the boy who leads the way of the crucifix — this is the way of all who do good and are charitable and who give to others — just like the fragrance, the smell of good and justice adhere to one!"

*the parade where they carried a large crucifix from the church to the governor's house and back to the church.
**a stick wit fragrant herbs which they would burn to give off a good scent.

47

Do not tell lies.

Do not tell lies.
Even only one lie that leaves your lips will
blemish your name and that of your family
forever, because a liar is considered one who will
not hesitate to stick a dagger in his friend's back.
And as you must be careful of telling lies,
you must be careful of leaving out the truth
because truth is like the chameleon —
when it leaves your lips it can shroud itself
in the guise of a lie...

48

As well as you can look back.

As well as you can look back,
so you will do well in looking forward.

49

I will leave behind me.

I will leave behind me property, books and a tombstone... and their importance is nothing compared to the impression I shall leave on my descendants' hearts.

50

Every young lad and young lass.

Every young lad and young lass will do well to remember — choose your partners for the journey not according to their merits or skills, but according to their ability to watch your back for the entire length of your journey.

51

Keep the rules of man.

Keep the rules of man
as if they were God's rules,
and keep God's rules
as if they were man's rules. If your give
preference to one over the other,
you will end up not keeping any of the rules.

52

He who shouts the loudest.

He who shouts the loudest at the tribunal*
does not get justice.
He who gets justice is one who puts into words
the inner feelings and thoughts of the
members of the tribunal.

*a group of men of the cloth and village heads who acted as judges during the writer's time.

53

At the end of the day.

At the end of the day,
a son will behave according to his father's example, and not according to his council. In the battle between advice and personal example, there can be only one victor — personal example.

54

When you cannot act like a lion.

When you cannot act like a lion when faced by your enemy, act like a mouse who runs to hide from every enemy. Many triumph over enemies stronger than themselves by flight, and only few beat those stronger than them.
There is no shame in flight
and no honor in defeat —
only the end result of the way
determines its outcome.

55

One day, I went with my father.

One day, I went with my father to receive a plot of land to till. My father laid his bundle in the shade of the stone wall and turned towards the field, and I followed his lead. My father picked up a stone, turned around and walked in little steps back toward the stone wall, laid the stone down next to it and went back to the field to get another stone.
I did the same — stone after stone.
In an adjacent field, on the other side of the low stone wall, two young brothers worked to clear the land of stones and rocks.
At first, they tried to carry a load of stones and loaded each other's arms with many stones, which fell out on the way to the wall.
Afterwards, they tried throwing the stones — throw the stone, hurry to it, pick it up again, and threw it again to the base of the wall. And when they tired of throwing the stones, they tried carrying the stones on a tree trunk that they held between them.

All this time, I followed my father,
step by step, stone by stone.
By nightfall, our plot of land was ready for
tilling, and even though my arms and legs ached,
my heart was full of pride. The adjacent plot,
however, there were still scattered stones which
would ping against the plough.

56

It is easier to retrieve a stone.

It is easier to retrieve a stone that was thrown into the deep sea than it is to retrieve the word of a youth after it leaves his mouth.

57

The young man acts as if his success.

The young man acts as if his success depends on God —
and prays as if his success depends on himself.
The old man acts as if his success depends on himself —
and prays as if his success depends on God.

58

The young man.

The young man thinks that God is
in the church or on the cross.
The old man knows that Gods is
in all places
that open the door for him to come through.

59

The man at the oars during a storm.

The man at the oars during a storm raises his
eyes to the horizon and prays to his God...
but if he stops rowing,
he will meet his maker
at the bottom of the ocean.

60

As God knows what is best.

As God knows what is best
for the creatures he created from chaos,
so parents know what is good
for their offspring.

61

Many years ago, on the island of Malta.

Many years ago, on the island of Malta
there lived a woman who was known for her
suffering, on whose rounded shoulders all of the
world's suffering landed.
She was poor and sick, and married robbers
who were hanged on the gallows and she
was left with one son who fell to his death into
the sea from one of the cliffs.
Her fate was so bitter, that she was known
throughout the island of Malta as the
epitome of suffering — as if she were Job's twin.
Time went on and she hid a cruel robber in
her house. When the soldiers found him, she was
also taken to court and was sentenced
to be hanged.
And, as per the local custom, she was washed,
her hair was combed and cleaned, she was
dressed in fancy clothes and even had a feast
brought to her cell from the King's table.
As she walked to the gallows,
her face shined with joy.

When the King saw her, he wondered about her exultation. He ordered the guard to bring her before him and he asked her why she was so happy in her last moments.
And the woman answered:
"My King, I am 60 years old and I have never, until now, had a full stomach, combed hair and clean clothes. I am happy that all wishes have come true in my last moments."
The King ordered the woman to be pardoned, and that, as was the practice in those days,
to carve in stone at the entrance to his palace the following:

One moment of joy
balances out 100 years of sorrow.

62

Whoever knows his wine.

Whoever knows his wine and many years of wine-drinking, knows that the bottle does not reflect its contents.
He who sips his first wine, judges by the bottle and not by the smoothness on his palate.

63

When you climb the mountain.

When you climb the mountain,
it is best that you reach the top first.
When you tumble down the slope,
it is best that you be the last to fall
to the bottom.

64

A father who forgets his teacher.

A father who forgets his teacher,
even if he remembers all that he taught him,
will not have the power to teach
his son anything.

65

Manners, eloquence, poetry, music, art...

Manners, eloquence, poetry, music, art... culture separates enlightened man from the savage. And this culture is like a mirror — the more you polish it, gently and continuously, the more is will shine and be clear.
The polishing of youngsters is the study of their culture. The more they learn in humility and diligence, so their clarity and maturity will increase, as will the light emanating from them.
If the polishing of the youth is gentle, the mirror will be worthy of the king's palace.
If it is rough, the mirror will be worthy of a farmer's shack.
Remember this.

66

People depend on the Times.

People depend on the Times. All have not had the Age they deserved, and many who have met with it, have not nevertheless had the happiness to make the best use of it. Others have been worthy of a better Age; which is an argument, that everything that is good, does not always triumph. Things of this world have their season, and that which is most eminent is obnoxious to the freakishness of custom.

But it is always the comfort of a Young Wise Man, that he has a future. For if his own age be ungrateful to him, those that come after do him justice.

67

The path to the top.

The path to the top always passes through the ascent of the mountain.
If you turn towards the slope —
the easier to pass through —
you will never reach the top.

68

The young couple.

The young couple is always looking into each other's eyes.
The long-term couple always looks...
in the same direction!

69

Many youngsters believe that the way of life.

Many youngsters believe that the way of life
is thus — same goes with same; or more
poetically, the raven walks after its mate. Thus,
when youngsters look for their partners they will
look for those similar to themselves:
in age, look, status, etc. in order to get a
"match" as a couple.
But the older and wiser know that the glue that
holds the couple together is the differences,
and these differences do not particularly stem
from them being male and female.
Different goals and ways of acting are the glue
that holds them together.
Two people, different from one another can
match like a key does a lock.
Two people who "match" each other exactly are
likely to be like a couple of keys —
that without a lock do not have desire.

70

When I was a youth.

When I was a youth, one morning on my way to my study class in church, I ran into the village bully who was standing in the center of the wooden bridge that spans across the river that separates our house from the church where my class was. I left behind on that bridge both my dignity and my lunch, but I left with something big — a black eye! And there wasn't one friend of mine who didn't hear about the heroic battle that I fought against the bullies that attacked me! When I went back home, my face was swollen and my stomach was empty, and thus my father saw me. He heard my tale and then he turned to the wardrobe and retrieved his wide brimmed hat that shaded his face and ordered me to wear this hat until my face was back to normal. "Don't expose you're your wounds to the world because their eyes see the wound and not the body," he instructed me.

71

There is no youngster.

There is no youngster who can stand in front of the world as an independent being without the net that ties them to their parents, their family and their community.

72

Sometimes, silence is...

Sometimes,
silence is also
the lie
that you tell
yourself.

73

It is easier to mold others.

It is easier to mold others
in the figure of excellence...
than it is to mold yourself
to be excellent.

74

It is better for the youngster.

It is better for the youngster
to think of his disadvantages
when he is awake —
and to think of the disadvantages of others
when is asleep.

75

Remember — the taller the tree.

Remember —
the taller the tree,
the deeper its roots that it shoots
into the ground.

76

Hatred is a quality.

Hatred is a quality
of man.
Forgiveness is
a Divine quality.

77

A rotten plank of wood.

A rotten plank of wood in the fence
invites the thief.
A rotten plank of wood in a ship
invites the Angel of Death.

78

A dance with your partner.

A dance with your partner
adds joy to life...
unless you're dancing in a small boat
sailing on rough seas.

79

When you're on a path.

When you're on a path,
see the that you have already walked
and not the path that separates you
from your destination.

80

One day two farmers.

One day two farmers were walking in the city's market when they saw before them a stall with small clay jugs. The first one went up to the stall and examined the the clay jugs, immediately wrinkled his nose and pointed out the faults in the design of the jugs, the scratches and the bangs. But his friend, even though he heard his words, picked up a jug and looked inside it, and inside was the sweetest honey he had ever tasted. He immediately bought a jug to take home. And all the way home to their village, the first farmer complained that he hadn't found anything at the market to buy, and the other farmer was proud of the tasty honey that he had found at the same market.

He who sees the hidden behind the obvious, will taste the sweetness of honey.

81

Man divides into two types.

Man divides into two types:
those that want to be as alike as possible
to others, each according to who he chooses
to resemble;
and others that want to be different,
unique and separate from others.

The vineyard owner will always choose
the vine shoots to plant from the vine with full,
sweet bunches of grapes because he believes that
the son is like the father.
Only few will take the shoot from the vine
with poor bunches of grapes...
and many times, this particular shoot
will grow the perfect vine.

82

Remember, the mistake that you made.

Remember, the mistake that you made is a mistake. It isn't you, it isn't your essence. Youngsters often tend to believe that the deed reflects the essence: if you entered another's field and stole a basket of fruit — you are a thief! But reality is not like this. The theft is theft and deserves to be disgraced, but man, in his essence, is not a thief. The cloud of the theft hangs above his head and its seal has been stamped into him forever, but if he listens to his essence, he can still live a life of honesty and end his life as a decent person.

People create bad deeds.
Bad deeds do not create people.

83

The power of the individual.

The power of the individual id measured
in the number of times he can fail
and still remain himself.

84

He who lifts his eyes only to the treetops.

He who lifts his eyes only to the treetops and mountaintops, will find himself scuffing his legs with the stones along the way.

85

Never hire a worker.

Never hire a worker to hoe your lot
if that same worker eats his meals
before he has one bead of sweat
on his brow.

86

In the summer.

In the summer, when they grind the grain, each farmer is quick to greet the owner of the mill. This is the way of the world. If you need something, the man holding the desired item is enlightened in your eyes. Remember this when you raise your eyes to others... and especially if you are he that holds the key needed for the benefit of others.

87

Don't look for a friend.

Don't look for a friend who always agrees with you, who laughs when you laugh and who cries when you cry. For this purpose, it is enough to find a polished mirror.

88

The more blunt and outspoken you are.

The more blunt and outspoken you are
about your opinions,
the less people you will find
who agree with you.

89

When you are angry.

When you are angry with a partner or a friend
you are not punishing him...
you are punishing yourself.

90

Never read all of an author's books

Never read all of an author's books, never listen to all of a musician's music, and never taste all the vats of wine in a vineyard. Leave yourself something you haven't read, haven't heard and haven't tasted, and you shall have a reason for the passion to read another book, listen to another song and taste another glass of wine.
For what is the essence of a man's life?
To yearn for the familiar that he hasn't yet known. When you read an unfamiliar book of an author whose other books you have read, you will feel as if you have returned to the garden whose paths you know from childhood. When you hear a new song of a musician whose work you know, you will feel as if you have returned to your childhood. When you taste of the vat of wine that you have been yearning for for years, you will taste a hint of the wine served to kings.
Leave something for later — never extinguish your passion because passion is the flame that keeps the fire burning in the heart of the youth.

91

The clever man fixes the hole in the roof

The clever man fixes the hole in the roof
of his house before the rains fall.
The stupid man fixes the hole in the roof
of his house after his house
has been flooded with rain.

This is the nature of man,
and the hole in the roof tells us
about his wisdom or stupidity.

92

If you do not know how to swim

If you do not know how to swim — don't jump into the turbulent water to save a drowning man. When you know how to swim, jumping into the turbulent water is a brave and noble act. When you do not know how to swim, the same act is an act of stupidity that will lead to your loss and will not help the drowning person. Stay in a safe place, call for help or throw a rope to save the person drowning.

Even better — learn how to swim!

93

If you don't want to soil your clothes

If you don't want to soil your clothes
with mud —
don't choose the muddy path.

If you don't want to be hurt
by the bad nature of some —
don't choose the path of the wrongdoers.

94

Often, you learn the value of something...

Often, you learn the value of something...
only after it has been broken.
So it is with a clay jug,
and so it is with the King's scepter.

95

One jump after another

One jump after another will take you a short distance in the blink of an eye. So is the way of the youth to cover distances, because their eyes do not see far into the distance, and the end of the way always appears to them within reach.
Step by step —
this is the way of the adult
to pass long distances,
because they can see the end of the way
and they know that it is as long as
a person's lifetime.

96

Look around you

Look around you. People resemble one another like ants in an anthill.
Even if you compare a man to a woman, a youth to the elderly, a tall person to a short one — you will see that the resemblance between them is great and that the difference barely exists.
Similarity is the bridge that connects all people, like ants in a nest or bees in a hive.
How are people different to each other?
In deeds.
Because the differences are in their deeds, and there are those who are at the top of the mountain, while others are buried at eh bottom of a pit.
And man is valued by his deeds.

97

To he who has been walking in the desert

To he who has been walking in the desert, a lot of water will seem like heaven on earth, but the same desert will seem like heaven on earth to the drowning man who is using the last of his strength to stay afloat in a lot of water.

98

The higher you climb

The higher you climb
to the top of tree,
the harder the fall
to the ground.

99

A young man

A young man
must carve the following motto
onto his heart:

lead your life thus
that you would be happy
to be your own best friend.

100

A man can change his name

A man can change his name,
move house,
work at a new profession
and exchange his nobleman's clothes
for those of a jester.

The only thing he cannot change is…
his past.

101

A young man must look towards

A young man must look towards
the honorable and not to the dishonorable,
to the lofty and not to the lowness.
It is not easy.
Often, it is easier for the young boy to mimic
that closest to him and to see in that person an
honorable character worth emulating —
and the youth will always that closest to him
better than that further away from him.

Learning to differentiate
the worthy from the unworthy
is how the youth becomes a man.

102

The young girl must remember

The young girl must remember that
even if she is as pretty as a rose...
the time will come when she must start
to blossom.
A bud cannot remain a bud forever.

Blossoming is the only way to bear —
as time goes by —
fruit.

103

The young man who has not learned

The young man who has not learned
the wisdom of his elders,
will believe that his house
is the biggest house
and his wife
is the most beautiful of all women.

But

If luck has smiled on him
and he is rich,
he will believe that his house is small
and his wife,
ugly.

104

A stiff rod

Often,
a stiff rod
can explain things
better than
a soft word
can.

105

Whenever a disaster befell our family

Whenever a disaster befell our family,
my mother would run to the city center
and keen there for hours and days,
involving the entire community in her disaster.
And on other days,
when joyous events visited us,
she would cover our estate with tables
laden with treats,
and every man — near or far —
was invited to partake in the celebration.

And this we learned from her: involve others in your sorrows, because even if your sorrow is as high as a mountain, among many it will look like a hill; and involve others in your joys, because even if it is a drop in the ocean, the happiness will swell like Noah's deluge when
it is among others.

106

A man's generosity is measured

A man's generosity is measured by looking at the doors of his house: he whose doors are wide open and people come in and out during feasts and celebrations, will earn the reputation of a generous man... in the eyes of fools!
Because the wise will look to see who passes through the door during feasts and celebrations, the poor and the impoverished and the wealthy and noble, generous is the owner of the house.

But if those entering his door one after another alight from luxury coaches and march in in all their pomp and glory,
even if there are many of them —
the owner of the house does not know generosity.

107

When you hear or see a young man

When you hear or see a young man arguing
or fighting with a friend,
you can see how he was raised at home.

108

Respect is often man's main property

Respect is often man's main property,
even though it doesn't have a price
and it cannot be traded in the city market.
And my mother taught me that love is like
respect — it cannot be traded in markets and it
cannot be bought for any amount of money.

109

He who is unable to love

He who is unable to love himself, is incapable of loving others!

110

We live in a world

We live in a world where things are traded,
something for something else.
The olive grower will give his neighbor, the
vineyard owner, a jug of olive oil and will receive
in return a jug of wine.
The farmer gives the shoemaker a silver coin
and in return receives a pair of shoes.
But when we give others a compliment,
a supportive shoulder,
encouragement or love —
we must not expect anything in return.
A compliment said
with the expectation of something in return
has in it a drop of poisonous venom.

111

If you call your son stupid

If you call your son stupid and your daughter a tramp — people will believe you!

112

If you studied the bible a lot

If you studied the bible a lot —
your return will be great.
And in a modern society,
he whose return is low,
hasn't ever studied the bible.

Study.

And if your youth has passed
without the bible —
teach it to your children.

113

I have never seen

I have never seen
an elephant chasing a fly
to try and crush it...

114

The question is the path to understanding

The question is the path to understanding.
Understanding is the key to action.
Therefore, learn this in your youth:
ask those wiser than yourself in order
to understand,
and realize your understanding
through your deeds
in order to fulfill your purpose.

115

Even the staunchest believer

Even the staunchest believer locks the gates to his home at night.

116

The wisdom of the wise

The wisdom of the wise is…

the ability to hide it from the evil eye and from the envy of others.

117

If you remember the beating

If you remember the beating that you received even after it has healed, the pain will be with you for the rest of your life.

118

The smell of garbage

The smell of garbage emanating from your neighbor's yard will always be stronger than the smell of garbage emanating from your own backyard.

A scratch on your arm from a nail will always be more painful than a knife wound in your neighbor's thigh.

A new scarf will always be more colorful on your neighbor's shoulders than on your own shoulders.

The food on your mother's table will always be tastier than that in your neighbor's house… but if you eat the same food at an inn and pay a high price for it, its flavor will be the tastiest of all.

And remember: **man is close to himself**.

119

The guide who leads with a confident step

The guide who leads with a confident step, will lead confident people.

The guide who leads with a faltering step, will find hesitant people behind him.

120

The young boy sees

The young boy sees that that is close to him with his eyes and that that is further from him, far over the horizon, with his spirit.

A young man sees that that is close to him through the eyes of his patron or teacher and that that is further from him, beyond the horizon, with his own eyes.

And with the years, the old man sees that that is close to him through the clouds of reality and that that is far from him is nothing but a shapeless glow.

121

When I turned 14 years old

When I turned 14 years old I went with my father to visit my uncle who lived in a distant village. When we set out, we took a bottle of wine and a loaf of bread and I placed a short knife in my pocket. My father took nothing in his pockets except a needle and thread. If you wish, this is the wisdom of the man.

122

In my youth

In my youth, I asked my father how
to choose my friends,
and his answer was short:
choose those whose visit makes you happy.
Stay away from those that make you happy…
when they leave.

123

A boy or girl become adults

A boy or girl become adults when they deepen their roots in the reality of their lives so much so that even the strongest wind will not knock them to the ground. Because the wind is like man's destiny, and only he who can bear the gusts of wind without being uprooted, will survive.

124

You cannot build a house

You cannot build a house
with a sword.
You cannot wage war
with a hammer.

125

When you are single

When you are single and past the teen years, time passes much more slowly than the time of married people and those with families.

126

A pothole in the road

A pothole in the road is a mirror
of man's character.
The even-tempered man who sees the pothole,
measures his step and sidesteps it either to the
left or to the right.
The man who's looking for a challenge, jumps
over it and walks on feeling that he has beaten
the elements of nature.
The man who is looking for quarrels will go out
of his way to find the owner of that road and,
whether it be the owner of the estate bordering
the road or the head of the village, he will
complain to him about this terrible obstacle.

Only the enlightened man will go off the path,
collect some sand and will fill in the pothole,
and pat down the earth with his feet.

127

One mistake can never correct another

One mistake can never correct another. When I was child, my father sent me with a knife to cut down the vines. In my inexperience, I made a mistake and cut one of them too low down. In fear of my father's anger I went back and cut all the vines that I had already cut to the height of the one that I had cut too low by mistake.

And thus I left behind me a trail of errors, and there has never been a mistake that can fix one that I made before.

128

On his way to the woods

On his way to the woods to hunt wild animals, the hunter carries his bow in his hand like it were his son.

On his return home from the woods, he carries his kill in his arms and his bow on his back, as if it were a bundle of kindling wood.

129

When walking on a path

When walking on a path,
you can walk either
in the light or the shade.
So it is when you walk
the path of belief.

130

The seed of fear

The seed of
fear
is sown much deeper in man's mind than
the seed of
hope.

131

It is natural that the blind admiration

It is natural that the blind admiration of a young man will turn into blind love.
And there are those who claim it is true when he is a youth —
and doubly true when it is a young girl.

So are born the fools,
of which there are many among the young.

The nature of the passing years and the close familiarity make one temper the admiration, which leads to the dissipation of the blindness... and the disappearance of the fools.

132

Pretty words

Pretty words, good language and eloquent speech are the beauty aids of the young boys and girls. If we hear eloquent speech without seeing the speaker, we will give the anonymous speaker all the good qualities that we would like to see in ourselves. If we hear stuttering speech without seeing the speaker, we will give that speaker all the bad qualities that that we wouldn't want to find in ourselves.
Eloquent speech is born through listening. Learn to listen to your parents, your teachers and your friends and you will find the path to eloquent speech.

133

As the lit candle

As the lit candle gets shorter,
so grows its light.

134

If you made a mistake

If you made a mistake
and you haven't corrected it —
you have made two mistakes.

135

The father closes the hole in the bucket

The father closes the hole in the bucket
before he fills it.
The son closes the hole in the bucket
after all the water has run out of it.

136

The great philosophers of Ancient times

The great philosophers of Ancient times used to talk to their reflection in the water, and only after honing their words, would they turn to their students. It is worth it for the young man to learn this custom when he needs to weigh his thoughts.

137

With the years

With the years, man learns
to look forward with hope...
and to look to the sides
with love.
But the failure of many people,
like the failure of Lot's wife,
is to look back
and to see everything.

138

Leaves that have fallen

Leaves that have fallen from the tree
blow in the wind.
Fish that have died
are carried away by the current.
Even the highest mountain cannot remain thus
against the wind that blows day after day.
And learn from this —
without living, you cannot stay in your place.

139

In order to see the stars

In order to see the stars
you need, first and foremost...
darkness.

140

Man's years on earth are numbered

Man's years on earth are numbered,
for the child in its cot
and for the elderly in their sickbeds,
for the one they are numbered
and for the other the years are many...
but the years of death
are not numbered for anyone.

141

Man lives within boundaries

Man lives within boundaries.
His skin is the boundary of his body.
The walls are the boundary of his house.
Fences are the boundary of his estate.
Stepping stones are the boundary of his district.
Flags are the boundary of his country.
Everything in man's world has
some type of boundary —
except for the words
that leave his mouth,
which have no boundaries.

142

No man has ever made loneliness

No man has ever made loneliness his goal in life, be it the man chasing after pleasures or the suffering monk. Man is alone only at the moment of his birth — and of his death.

143

The tiniest spark

The tiniest spark
can set alight
the biggest of forests.

A tiny hole
will empty
the largest vat of wine.

A thin beam of light
will light up
the darkest dungeon.

And one good deed
can save the entire world,
even if it is a trivial deed.

144

Stopping is the largest obstacle

Stopping is the largest obstacle to those walking.
An unrelenting tortoise will get farther
than the deer who stops after each spring.

And remember that stopping
is the first step to
turning back...

145

Shortcuts will bring the youth

Shortcuts will bring the youth
to a destination
that he didn't want to reach.

146

A young man expresses his pain

A young man expresses his pain,
his rage and his frustration
by screaming,
and the louder the scream the stronger the pain.

An old man expresses his pain,
his rage and his frustrations
through silence,
and the silence is louder than any scream.

147

The sapling of a pine tree

The sapling of a pine tree will grow into a mighty tree under the sun's rays. Place a shade over it and it will wither and die.
A young boy grows and becomes a respected man in the shadow of an older patron, be it his father, his uncle or his teacher. If this shadow is taken away, his source of vitality will dry up.

148

A young man

A young man, even if he goes up the mountain via a thousand different paths, will always look down and see the same view, whether it be in winter or in summer, during a storm or in the spring.

An old man, even if he goes up the mountain via the same path time after time, will see a different view every time he looks down.

149

It is better if the strict father

It is better if the strict father observe the baby birds in the nest — they seem to be defenseless and helpless and are constantly voicing their needs through chirps and pushing. But the moment these chick spread their wings, you'll never know how far they can actually fly.
See your offspring as chicks within the four walls of your home, and in your later years you will witness them soaring up high like eagles.

150

The tracks that the adult leaves

The tracks that the adult leaves
are signs of the burden of the days
he has left behind.

151

When you fall off the roof

When you fall off the roof of a house,
a thump on the backside
seems like a kiss on the forehead.

152

It is hard for a man

It is hard for a man to admit to his faults.
It is even harder to leave them behind.

153

It is impossible not to learn

It is impossible not to learn anything,
be it as small as the eye of the needle,
when you open a book.

154

Through a telescope* you can see things in the distance as if they are near.
Using a lantern you can find a coin even in the darkest night.
Make it a habit to keep the wisdom, that which helps to see the hidden as revealed, and it will serve you like both a lantern and a telescope.

*The earliest evidence of working telescopes were the refracting telescopes that appeared in the Netherlands in 1608. Their development is credited to three individuals: Hans Lippershey and Zacharias Janssen, who were spectacle makers in Middelburg, and Jacob Metius of Alkmaar.

155

There are people who find treasures

There are people who find treasures in every field
and forest — fruit on a tree branch,
a mushroom growing in the brush or
a beautiful flower to bring to a loved one.
And there are people that cannot see
any treasure in either fruit groves
or in the abundant field.
The ability to find treasures everywhere,
to find the grain in a haystack,
is the ability of the man who
knows how to value his life properly.

156

The truth

The truth
has no brothers or sisters.
It is an only child —
the one and only.

157

If you light a lantern

If you light a lantern in the heart of a forest
at daytime,
it would simply be a waste of precious oil.
But the light of the lantern will be
like the sun in your eyes
in the dark night.

So you should rule your life —
try to be the light where there is darkness,
and not to be a spot of light in a place
where your light is not seen.

158

Amongst the elderly

Amongst the elderly there are many more seekers of the truth and of reconciliation than the number of warmongers and quarrelmakers. The nature of peace is such that it leads to longevity, and the nature of war to shorter life spans, to both he who lost the war and he who won the war.

159

Every young boy and young girl

Every young boy and young girl
have friends
who always smile at them and praise them.
But the true friend
is the one who praises him...
behind his back!

160

A father should learn

A father should learn to treat his offspring
as a leader treats his followers —
not to force them to join you,
but invite them to accompany you on a journey.

161

Remember, son

Remember, son —
the best mirror to look at
is the friend
who has stayed true
both through the good and the bad.

162

A youngster's season

A youngster's season
is like the season of the fruit tree —
when the colorful and fragrant blossoms
disappear,
the nourishing fruit
takes its place.

163

Remember that the view of the world

Remember that the view of the world
that you see
is nothing but your image
reflected in the mirror of your soul.

164

Every morning

Every morning, my father used to mend the stone wall surrounding our property — replacing a stone that fell from its place, removing a weed from the cracks or raising the sand heaps the wall rest on. He always claimed that one should nurture good relations with one's neighbors, and there's nothing better than a good solid stone wall to maintain good neighborly relations...

165

Even if you try to be somebody else

Even if you try to be
somebody else,
you will never be able to
not be yourself.

166

Never urinate on your friend's doorstep

Never urinate on your friend's doorstep...
unless his house is on fire!

167

The first step

The first step determines
the length,
the direction
and the pace
of the entire journey.

168

The young man who asks for

The young man who asks for his
sweetheart's love and is rejected by her,
feels like a complete fool...
for a day, a week, a month...
The young man who doesn't even try
to get his sweetheart's love
because he's shy or for some other reason —
will feel like a fool for the rest of his life.

169

A small boy

A small boy
who is afraid of the dark
gets a hug.

An adult man
who is afraid of the dark
gets derision.

170

An hour spent

An hour spent in joy, feels like a minute;
An hour spent worrying, feels like eternity.

171

A man with a noble soul

A man with a noble soul —
all of his words and deeds will be noble.
But a man who speaks nobly and acts nobly
is not always noble,
because sometimes a man behaves nobly
even though it isn't in his nature,
but because he wants
to attain some advantage in his life.

172

When looking for a teacher

When looking for a teacher for your children, do
not evaluate the teacher
who comes to offer his services,
but go out and evaluate his former students.

173

Whoever stands on the shoulders

Whoever stands on the shoulders of someone bigger than him —
be it his father, his teacher or his patron —
will always see farther than him.

174

You cannot make a true new friend

You cannot make a true new friend in an hour...
but you can lose your best friend in a moment.

To ascend to the top of a tower
takes hundreds of stairs...
to fall from the top of the tower
takes only one small step!

175

Laziness is a bad trait

Laziness is a bad trait
when it accompanies a deed.
But when laziness accompanies speech,
it brings silence —
and this is its great blessing.

176

Even if you walk a whole day

Even if you walk a whole day with a hole in your pocket through which your pouch of coins fell through, you won't feel its absence unless you look for the coin to pay for your meal at the inn.

177

It is easier to believe

It is easier to believe
a lie
than it is to open your heart
to the truth.

178

The closer you are

The closer you are
to the truth,
the more afraid of it
you become.

179

A lone wolf

A lone wolf will always look for the pack.

Even if you meet
a lone wolf in the mountains —
look around for the pack
because even a lone wolf
will go to the pack,
or has just left it.

180

Truth

Truth is preferred over love.

181

A hen that lays an egg

A hen that lays an egg
in the ducks' enclosure,
mustn't be surprised
if her chicks are ducklings.

182

An ignorant person

An ignorant person is
he who puts his hand
into the fire
to get a glowing piece of coal.

A clever person would never do that.

Therefore, ignorant people do deeds
that clever people would never do.

183

Whenever my father gave a coin

Whenever my father gave a coin of charity
to a beggar, he would avert his eyes.
When I asked him about this
he said that he was embarrassed to see
the shame in the beggar's eyes.

184

Ignorance

Ignorance is like a fake silver coin —
it passes from hand to hand
and all who have it,
think it is a coin of value.

185

The light of one candle

The light of one candle
banishes great darkness.
The wisdom of one man
lights the way to an entire village.

186

A lie is like olive oil

A lie is like olive oil.
The truth is like a spring...
and no matter how much you
mix the two,
the oil will always float
on top of the water.

187

A man is king at the table

A man is king at the table in his own home, a
woman is like a queen
and their children
sitting with them at the table
are princes and princesses.

And that is why it is said:
The table in a man's home is bigger
than the king's table
in his castle that is walled in.

188

A silly youth

A silly youth interrupts his friend
and doesn't let him
get three words in a row out of his mouth.

The wiser he gets,
the more he'll learn to value his silences,
and then he will learn
to hear his friend's words.

189

The nature of a door

The nature of a door is
that you can enter a house through it...
as well as leave through it.

190

An honest man

An honest man does not know
the names
of the judges and lawyers in his city.

The swindler is the one who takes pride
in his familiarity with
the representatives of the law.

191

If you are looking for

If you are looking for a wise councilor —
choose the one who uses words sparingly,
because unnecessary words
are like water to soup —
when you add too much of it,
the soup will taste watery.

192

A misunderstanding

A misunderstanding is the most common cause of conflicts, arguments and quarrels. See reality through clear eyes and a pure soul, and you will avoid many quarrels.

193

Opportunities knock

Opportunities knock on a man's door,
but that is only when he has a door
with oiled hinges
and which is open wide to all.

194

Sometimes the best way

Sometimes the best way of knowing
what to expect on your journey...
is to ask those
who have gone before you.

195

Even the best fruit

Even the best fruit,
if left on the shelf too long,
will rot.

196

The tyrant

The tyrant plants trees at the entrance
to his palace in the hope that he will live
long enough to see his enemies hanging
from the branches of these trees.

The nobleman plants trees at the entrance
to his palace in the hope that he will live
long enough to see the people in his community
eating the fruit off these trees
and sitting in their shade.

197

He who walks behind

He who walks behind a donkey,
must not complain
about the kicks he receives.

198

Stupidity

Stupidity is a disease
that if you catch it when you're young,
you will not be cured of it
even in your old age.

199

Young man

Young man, it is better for you to surround yourself with clever people, even if you feel inferior to them, and not with stupid people, even if you feel better than them.

Because he who sees wisdom will be wise, and he who sees stupidity will be stupid.

200

Close your eyes

Close your eyes —
and you turn light into darkness.

Open your eyes —
and you turn dark into light.

Release your will
and bad turns to good.

Imprison your will
and good turns into bad.

201

Memory

Memory last longer than man's life.

202

The wise

The wise are like a fire burning in an oven —
spreading light and heat,
and everything nearby
gets what it deserves.

But you must remember —
he who puts his hand in the fire,
will get burned,
and like him,
he who puts his burden on the wise
because wisdom may be like burning coals,
that if placed outside the oven
will cause a great fire.

203

Every man

Every man should bless the reign
under which he lives.
For without the fear for this reign,
people would be killing one another
in the city streets.

204

He who learns from the youth

He who learns from the youth is like the man who drinks his wine straight from the press, before the wine has soaked up the flavor from the vat.

He who learns from the aged is like the man who drinks his wine straight from the vat where the wine has been for many years — and whose flavor has improved.

205

The young man

The young man rides his horse for a long way in the summer heat, and upon reaching the spring drinks from its water, washes his face and hands and cools his feet in the water. And if he remembers, will water his horse as well.

The older man who reaches the spring, wipes his horse's sweat, gives it to drink and only then quenches his own thirst.

Thus on the road you see many young men sitting and moaning next to their horses whose legs have given in from the hard journey...
but the older man reaches his destination safely, he and his horse.

206

A crisis

A crisis is the axe that lands on a youth's love. Crisis is the glue that seals adults' love.

207

It is better for the young

It is better for the young man
to hang from a lion's tail
and not from a wolf's head.